Deion Sanders

A Biography: The Phenomenal Life of

a Two-Sport Superstar

Melissa B. Quintana

TABLE OF CONTENTS

INTRODUCTION

CHAPTER ONE: Early Life and Background

CHAPTER TWO: College Football Career

CHAPTER THREE: NFL Career

CHAPTER FOUR: Baseball Career

CHAPTER FIVE: Achievements and Awards

CHAPTER SIX: Personal Life

CHAPTER SEVEN: Controversies

CONCLUSION

INTRODUCTION

Deion Luwynn Sanders Sr. (born August 9, 1967), nicknamed "Prime Time" and "Neon Deion," is an American football coach and former player who is the current head football coach at the University of Colorado Boulder. He played college football at Florida State University, where he was a two-time All-American in football and a two-time All-American in track and field. He was drafted by the Atlanta Falcons in the first round of the 1989 NFL Draft, and he also played for the San Francisco 49ers, Dallas Cowboys, Washington Redskins, Baltimore Ravens, and New York Yankees.

Sanders is widely considered to be one of the greatest defensive backs in NFL history. He was a nine-time Pro Bowl selection, eight-time All-Pro selection, and was named the NFL Defensive Player of the Year in 1994. He also won two Super Bowls with the 49ers and Cowboys.

In addition to his NFL career, Sanders also played professional baseball. He was drafted by the New York Yankees in the 1988 amateur draft, and he played in the major leagues from 1989 to 1993. He was a two-time All-Star, and he helped the Braves win the World Series in 1992.

Sanders is a two-sport Hall of Famer, having been inducted into the Pro Football Hall of Fame in 2011 and the National Baseball Hall of Fame in 2021. He is also a member of the College Football Hall of Fame.

Sanders is known for his flamboyant personality and his flashy style of play. He was one of the first NFL players to wear his socks high, and he often dyed his hair different colors. He was also known for his trash-talking, and he was often involved in on-field altercations.

CHAPTER ONE: Early Life and Background

Deion Luwynn Sanders was born on August 9, 1967, in Fort Myers, Florida. His parents, Connie and Willie Sanders, divorced when he was two years old. He was raised by his mother and her new husband, Willie Knight, whom Sanders credits with being influential in his life.

Sanders was a natural athlete from a young age. He began playing organized baseball and football at the age of eight. In high school, he was a letterman and All-State honoree in football, basketball, and baseball. He was also named to the Florida High School Association

All-Century Team, which selected the top 33 players in the 100-year history of high school football in the state.

After high school, Sanders enrolled at Florida State University, where he played three sports for the Florida State Seminoles: football, baseball, and track. Beginning in his freshman year, he started in the Seminoles' secondary, played outfield for the baseball team that finished fifth in the nation, and helped lead the track and field team to a conference championship.

As a football player, Sanders was a two-time All-American and the winner of the 1988 Jim Thorpe Award, which is given to the best defensive back in college football. He also played in the 1989 Sugar Bowl, where he returned a punt 80 yards for a touchdown.

After his junior year of college, Sanders was drafted by the Atlanta Falcons in the first round of the NFL draft. He quickly became one of the best cornerbacks in the league, earning All-Pro honors five times and being named to the Pro Bowl nine times. He also won two Super Bowls with the Falcons (1995) and the Dallas Cowboys (1996).

In addition to his NFL career, Sanders also played Major League Baseball. He was drafted by the Kansas City Royals in the sixth round of the 1985 draft, but he did not sign with the team. He later played for the Atlanta Braves (1991-1992), San Francisco Giants (1993), and Baltimore Orioles (1996). He was named to the All-Star team in 1992.

Sanders retired from professional sports in 2006. He has since worked as a television analyst for the NFL Network and the SEC Network. He is also the head coach of Jackson State University's football team.

Sanders is considered one of the greatest athletes of all time. He was inducted into the Pro Football Hall of Fame in 2011 and the College Football Hall of Fame in 2013. He is also a member of the Florida Sports Hall of

Fame and the Florida State University Hall of Fame.

Despite his sometimes controversial personality, Sanders is widely respected for his athletic ability and his commitment to excellence. He is an inspiration to many young athletes, and he is considered one of the greatest sports figures of his generation.

CHAPTER TWO: College Football Career

Deion Sanders' college football career at Florida State University was nothing short of legendary. He was a two-time All-American, a two-time winner of the Jim Thorpe Award as the nation's top defensive back, and a member of the 1988 national championship team.

Sanders was a dynamic playmaker who could do it all on the defensive side of the ball. He was a shutdown corner who could lock down opposing receivers, and he was also a dangerous punt returner who could take it to the house at any time. In his three seasons at

Florida State, he intercepted 14 passes and returned three for touchdowns. He also returned 32 punts for 576 yards and two touchdowns.

Sanders' impact on the game was undeniable. He was named the Defensive MVP of the 1988 Sugar Bowl, in which Florida State defeated Auburn to win the national championship. He was also a finalist for the Heisman Trophy, finishing eighth in the voting.

After his college career, Sanders was drafted by the Atlanta Falcons in the first round of the 1989 NFL Draft. He went on to have a Hall of Fame career in the NFL, playing for the

Falcons, San Francisco 49ers, Dallas Cowboys, Washington Redskins, and Baltimore Ravens. He won two Super Bowls, was named to eight Pro Bowls, and was selected to the NFL's 75th Anniversary All-Time Team.

Sanders' college football career was a preview of the greatness that was to come in the NFL. He was a once-in-a-generation talent who helped to redefine the game of football. His legacy is secure as one of the greatest players to ever play the game.

Here are some of Deion Sanders' most notable accomplishments in college football:

* Two-time All-American (1987, 1988)

* Two-time winner of the Jim Thorpe Award (1987, 1988)

* Member of the 1988 national championship team

* Defensive MVP of the 1988 Sugar Bowl

* Heisman Trophy finalist (1988)

* Led the nation in punt return average in 1988 (15.2 yards per return)

* Broke Florida State's career punt return record with 753 yards

Sanders' college football career is one of the most decorated in history. He was a dominant force on the defensive side of the ball, and he also made a significant impact as a punt returner. He helped to lead Florida State to a national championship, and he was named one of the best players in college football history.

CHAPTER THREE: NFL Career

Deion Sanders, nicknamed "Prime Time," was one of the most versatile and exciting players in NFL history. He played cornerback, wide receiver, and punt returner, and he was a two-time Super Bowl champion.

Sanders was born in Fort Myers, Florida, in 1967. He played college football at Florida State University, where he was a two-time All-American. He was also the recipient of the Jim Thorpe Award as the nation's best defensive back in 1988.

The Atlanta Falcons drafted Sanders fifth overall in the 1989 NFL Draft. He quickly established himself as one of the best cornerbacks in the league, making the Pro Bowl in his rookie season. He also returned punts and kickoffs, and he scored two touchdowns on punt returns in 1989.

In 1994, Sanders signed with the San Francisco 49ers. He helped the 49ers win Super Bowl XXIX that season, and he was named the NFL Defensive Player of the Year.

After one season with the 49ers, Sanders signed with the Dallas Cowboys. He helped the Cowboys win Super Bowl XXX in 1996.

Sanders played for the Washington Redskins from 2000 to 2001, and he finished his NFL career with the Baltimore Ravens in 2004 and 2005.

Sanders retired from the NFL with 53 interceptions, 22 touchdowns, and 10,807 all-purpose yards. He was inducted into the Pro Football Hall of Fame in 2011.

In addition to his NFL career, Sanders also played professional baseball for nine seasons. He played for the New York Yankees, Atlanta Braves, Cincinnati Reds, and San Francisco Giants. He was a two-time All-Star in baseball.

Sanders was a larger-than-life figure who was known for his flamboyant personality and his flashy style of play. He was also a very talented athlete who was one of the best players in both the NFL and MLB. He is considered one of the greatest athletes of all time.

Here are some of Deion Sanders's NFL career highlights:

* 8x Pro Bowl selection
* 6x First-team All-Pro selection
* NFL Defensive Player of the Year (1994)
* 2x Super Bowl champion (1994, 1996)
* 53 interceptions (22nd all-time)
* 22 touchdowns (10th all-time)
* 10,807 all-purpose yards (23rd all-time)

Deion Sanders was a truly unique and special player. He was a dominant force on both sides of the ball, and he was one of the most exciting players to watch in NFL history. He is a true legend of the game.

Deion Sanders' Draft and Rookie Season

Deion Sanders was drafted by the Atlanta Falcons in the first round (fifth overall) of the 1989 NFL Draft. He was considered to be one of the most versatile athletes in the draft, and his speed and athleticism made him a highly sought-after prospect.

Sanders made an immediate impact in his rookie season, recording five interceptions, 39 tackles, one punt return for a touchdown, and even catching a pass on offense. He was named to the NFL All-Rookie Team and was also named the NFC Defensive Rookie of the Year.

One of Sanders' most memorable plays from his rookie season came in Week 10 against the New York Giants. On a fourth-and-10 play, Sanders intercepted a pass from Giants quarterback Phil Simms and returned it 90 yards for a touchdown. The play helped the Falcons win the game, 23-20.

Sanders' rookie season was a preview of the great things to come in his NFL career. He went on to play for five different teams in his 14-year career, and he was named to the Pro

Bowl eight times. He was also a two-time All-Pro selection and was inducted into the Pro Football Hall of Fame in 2011.

In addition to his NFL career, Sanders also played Major League Baseball. He was drafted by the Kansas City Royals in the sixth round of the 1985 draft, but he did not sign with them. He was later drafted by the New York Yankees in the 30th round of the 1988 draft, and he played for the Yankees, Atlanta Braves, Cincinnati Reds, and San Francisco Giants.

Sanders was a two-sport star who excelled at both football and baseball. He was one of the most exciting and dynamic players of his era, and he helped to change the way the game was played. His rookie season was just a glimpse of the greatness that was to come.

Here are some other notable stats from Sanders' rookie season:

* He led the NFL with 22 punt return yards per attempt.
* He was named to the Pro Football Weekly All-NFC Team.
* He was one of three rookies named to the Associated Press All-Rookie Team.

Sanders' rookie season was a historic one, and it helped to cement his place as one of the greatest athletes of all time. He was a true force of nature on the field, and he changed the way the game was played. His legacy will live on for generations to come.

Dallas Cowboys

Deion Sanders' stay with the Dallas Cowboys was brief, but it was memorable. He joined the team in 1995 after four seasons with the San Francisco 49ers, and he quickly became one of the most feared defenders in the NFL. He was named to the Pro Bowl in each of his five seasons with the Cowboys, and he was a key contributor to their Super Bowl XXX victory in 1996.

Sanders was a versatile player who could play both cornerback and punt returner. He was known for his speed and athleticism, and he was often called "Prime Time" for his showmanship on the field. He was also a flamboyant personality who was not afraid to speak his mind.

Sanders' time with the Cowboys came to an end in 2000, when he was released by the team. The Cowboys were trying to save money, and they felt that they could get similar production from other players. Sanders was disappointed by the move, but he went on to play two more seasons with the Washington Redskins before retiring.

Despite his short stay in Dallas, Sanders left a lasting impression on the Cowboys organization. He was a key part of their Super Bowl victory, and he helped to usher in a new era of success for the team. He is still considered one of the greatest cornerbacks of all time, and his time with the Cowboys is a part of his legacy.

Here are some of the highlights of Deion Sanders' time with the Dallas Cowboys:

* Named to the Pro Bowl in each of his five seasons with the team.
* Helped the Cowboys win Super Bowl XXX in 1996.
* Led the NFL in punt return yards in 1995.
* Named NFL Defensive Player of the Year in 1994.

* Recorded 26 interceptions in his five seasons with the Cowboys.

Deion Sanders is a Hall of Fame cornerback who had a successful career in both the NFL and Major League Baseball. His time with the Dallas Cowboys was brief, but it was memorable. He was a key part of their Super Bowl victory, and he helped to usher in a new era of success for the team. He is still considered one of the greatest cornerbacks of all time, and his time with the Cowboys is a part of his legacy.

As for whether or not Deion Sanders will ever coach the Cowboys, it seems unlikely. He has said in the past that he has no interest in coaching in the NFL, and he is currently the head coach of Jackson State University. However, anything is possible, and if the Cowboys ever do decide to offer him a coaching job, he would certainly be a hot commodity.

Deion Sanders was drafted by the Atlanta Falcons in the first round of the 1989 NFL Draft. He quickly became one of the best defensive players in the league, earning All-Pro honors in his first two seasons. He was also a dangerous punt and kickoff returner, scoring four touchdowns on returns in his rookie year.

In 1992, Sanders led the NFL in kickoff return yards and return touchdowns. He also had a career-high seven interceptions, returning one for a touchdown. The Falcons made the playoffs that year, but they lost in the NFC Championship Game to the Washington Redskins.

Sanders' best season with the Falcons came in 1993. He was named to his third Pro Bowl and led the league with five interceptions. He also returned two punts for touchdowns, one of which came in a Week 17 win over the New Orleans Saints that helped the Falcons clinch a playoff berth.

The Falcons made it to the Super Bowl that year, but they lost to the San Francisco 49ers. Sanders had a quiet game, recording no interceptions.

After the 1993 season, Sanders signed with the San Francisco 49ers. He won his first Super Bowl ring with the 49ers in 1994. He later won another Super Bowl ring with the Dallas Cowboys in 1996.

Sanders' time with the Falcons was brief, but he made a significant impact. He was one of the most exciting players in the NFL, and he helped the Falcons become a playoff contender. He is considered one of the greatest cornerbacks of all time.

Here are some of Deion Sanders' accomplishments during his time with the Atlanta Falcons:

* 3x Pro Bowl selection (1990, 1991, 1993)
* 2x First-team All-Pro selection (1990, 1991)
* NFL Leader in Kickoff Return Yards (1992)
* NFL Leader in Kickoff Return Touchdowns (1992)
* NFC Champion (1993)

Deion Sanders is a true NFL legend. He was a dominant force on both sides of the ball, and he helped the Falcons reach the Super Bowl. He is one of the most exciting players to ever play the game, and his legacy will be remembered for years to come.

Washington Football Team

Deion Sanders played for the Washington Redskins for one season in 2000. He was signed as a free agent after spending the previous five seasons with the Dallas Cowboys. Sanders was 33 years old at the time, but he was still one of the best cornerbacks in the NFL. He led the Redskins with five interceptions and was named to his eighth Pro Bowl.

Sanders's arrival in Washington was a major coup for the team. He was a two-time Super Bowl champion and one of the most flamboyant players in the NFL. He quickly became a fan favorite, and his presence helped to energize the Redskins' defense.

Sanders's best game of the season came in Week 10 against the Philadelphia Eagles. He returned an interception for a touchdown and also had a fumble recovery. The Redskins won the game 27-10, and Sanders was named the NFC Defensive Player of the Week.

The Redskins finished the season with a 9-7 record and missed the playoffs. However, Sanders's arrival was a positive sign for the team, and they were expected to be contenders in the years to come.

After the season, Sanders retired from the NFL. He finished his career with 53 interceptions, 19 fumble recoveries, and 10 touchdowns. He was inducted into the Pro Football Hall of Fame in 2011.

Sanders's impact on the Washington Redskins was significant. He was a lockdown cornerback who helped to transform the team's defense. He was also a major cultural force, and his presence helped to make the Redskins one of the most popular teams in the NFL.

Here are some of Deion Sanders's accomplishments with the Washington Redskins:

* Led the team with five interceptions

* Named to his eighth Pro Bowl

* Named NFC Defensive Player of the Week in Week 10

* Helped the Redskins finish the season with a 9-7 record

Deion Sanders is one of the greatest cornerbacks of all time. He played for four different teams in his career, but his one season with the Washington Redskins was a memorable one. He helped to transform the team's defense and made them one of the most popular teams in the NFL.

Baltimore Ravens

Deion Sanders played for the Baltimore Ravens in the 2004 and 2005 seasons. He was 37 years old at the time, and he had already played for four other NFL teams: the Atlanta Falcons, San Francisco 49ers, Dallas Cowboys, and Washington Redskins.

Sanders came out of retirement to play for the Ravens after being convinced by his friend Joe Zorovich, Ravens cornerback Corey Fuller, and linebacker Ray Lewis. He signed a one-year deal with the Ravens to be a nickelback. Sanders chose to wear the number 37, which matched his age at the time, to preemptively let people know that he was well aware of his relative senior status as an NFL player (additionally, the number 21, used by Sanders throughout his career, was already being worn by Ravens Pro Bowl cornerback Chris McAlister).

Sanders played in 16 games for the Ravens in 2004, recording 31 tackles and one interception. He also returned two punts for touchdowns. In 2005, Sanders played in 15 games, recording 25 tackles and one interception. He also returned one kickoff for a touchdown.

Sanders' most memorable moment as a Raven came in the 2004 playoffs. In the Divisional Round against the Pittsburgh Steelers, Sanders returned a punt 63 yards for a touchdown to help the Ravens win 27-10. The Ravens went on to win the Super Bowl that year, defeating the Philadelphia Eagles.

Sanders' time with the Ravens was brief, but it was certainly memorable. He was a valuable contributor to the team's Super Bowl victory, and he helped to solidify their reputation as one of the best defenses in the NFL.

In addition to his playing career, Sanders also had a successful stint as a television analyst. He worked for the NFL Network and ESPN, and he was known for his insightful commentary and his flamboyant personality.

Sanders is now retired from both football and television. He is currently the head football coach at the University of Colorado Boulder.

Here are some additional details about Deion Sanders' time with the Baltimore Ravens:

* He was the oldest player in the NFL in 2004.
* He was the only player in NFL history to play in both a Super Bowl and a World Series.
* He was inducted into the Pro Football Hall of Fame in 2011.
* He is considered to be one of the greatest defensive backs of all time.

Sanders' time with the Ravens was a brief but memorable one. He helped the team win a Super Bowl, and he cemented his legacy as one of the all-time greats.

CHAPTER FOUR: Baseball Career

Deion Sanders had a nine-year, part-time baseball career, playing left and center field in 641 games with four teams. He was drafted by the Kansas City Royals in the sixth round of the 1985 draft, but did not sign with them. The New York Yankees selected Sanders in the 30th round of the 1988 Major League Baseball draft, and he signed with the team on June 22. He batted . 284 in 28 minor league games after signing. The Yankees invited Sanders to spring training in 1989. Assigned to wear No. 71 as a uniform number, Sanders requested a single digit number. The Yankees gave him No. 2.

Sanders made his major league debut on May 31, 1989, at the age of 21. He appeared in 14 games for the Yankees that season, batting .158 with no home runs or RBIs. He was released by the Yankees after the season.

In 1991, Sanders signed with the Atlanta Braves. He had a breakout season, batting .263 with 14 triples, 29 stolen bases, and 46 runs scored. He was named to the National League All-Star team and finished 19th in the NL MVP voting.

Sanders continued to be a productive player for the Braves in 1992. He batted .277 with 10 triples, 36 stolen bases, and 60 runs scored. He also helped the Braves reach the World Series, where they lost to the Toronto Blue Jays in six games.

After the 1992 season, Sanders was traded to the Cincinnati Reds. He played two seasons with the Reds, batting .268 with 11 triples and 27 stolen bases in 1993 and .259 with 12 triples and 26 stolen bases in 1994.

In 1995, Sanders was traded to the San Francisco Giants. He played one season with the Giants, batting .262 with 10 triples and 21 stolen bases.

Sanders retired from baseball after the 1995 season. He finished his career with a .263 batting average, 101 triples, 186 stolen bases, and 464 runs scored. He was a two-time All-Star and a one-time World Series participant.

Sanders' baseball career was often overshadowed by his success in football. He was a two-time Super Bowl champion and a nine-time Pro Bowler. However, he was a legitimate major league talent and his accomplishments on the baseball diamond should not be overlooked. He was a rare athlete who was able to excel at the highest levels of two different sports.

In addition to his on-field accomplishments, Sanders was also known for his flamboyant personality and his flashy style of play. He was nicknamed "Prime Time" and "Neon

Deion" for his showmanship and his ability to make big plays. He was a popular figure with fans and media alike.

Deion Sanders' baseball career was brief, but it was memorable. He was a talented player who made a significant impact on the game. He is one of the few athletes who can claim to have played in both a Super Bowl and a World Series, and his dual-sport career is one of the most unique in sports history.

CHAPTER FIVE: Achievements and Awards

Deion Sanders is a Hall of Fame professional football and baseball player who is known for his flamboyant personality and his ability to play two sports at an elite level. He is the only athlete to play in both a Super Bowl and a World Series.

Sanders's NFL career began in 1989 with the Atlanta Falcons. He quickly established himself as one of the best cornerbacks in the league, earning eight Pro Bowl selections and six first-team All-Pro honors. He also returned punts and kickoffs for the Falcons, scoring eight touchdowns on returns.

In 1994, Sanders signed with the San Francisco 49ers. He helped the 49ers win Super Bowl XXIX that season, intercepting a pass in the game. He then signed with the Dallas Cowboys in 1995, and helped them win Super Bowl XXX the following year.

Sanders also played baseball during his NFL career. He was drafted by the New York Yankees in the second round of the 1988 MLB draft, and made his major league debut in 1989. He played for the Yankees, Atlanta Braves, Cincinnati Reds, and San Francisco Giants over the course of his nine-year baseball career.

Sanders retired from football in 2000 and from baseball in 2001. He was inducted into the Pro Football Hall of Fame in 2011 and the College Football Hall of Fame in 2013.

In addition to his on-field accomplishments, Sanders is also known for his flamboyant personality and his fashion sense. He has been nicknamed "Prime Time" and "Neon Deion" for his flashy style. He has also been a successful businessman, owning several businesses, including a clothing line and a sports management company.

Sanders is a true legend of sports. He is one of the most versatile athletes of all time, and he is one of the few players to have won championships in both the NFL and MLB. He is a role model for many young athletes, and he is an inspiration to anyone who has ever dreamed of achieving greatness.

Here is a list of Deion Sanders's most notable achievements and awards:

* Two-time Super Bowl champion (1994, 1995)
* Eight-time Pro Bowl selection
* Six-time first-team All-Pro
* Jim Thorpe Award winner (1988)
* College Football Hall of Fame inductee (2013)
* Pro Football Hall of Fame inductee (2011)
* MLB All-Star (1992)

* World Series champion (1992)

Sanders is a true icon of sports, and his achievements will be remembered for generations to come.

CHAPTER SIX: Personal Life

Deion Luwynn Sanders Sr. is a retired American football and baseball player who is currently the head football coach at the University of Colorado Boulder. He is a two-sport Hall of Famer, having been inducted into the Pro Football Hall of Fame in 2011 and the National Baseball Hall of Fame in 2021.

Sanders was born in Fort Myers, Florida, in 1967. He was a multisport star in high school, excelling in football, baseball, and track. He earned a scholarship to Florida State University, where he played both football and baseball. In football, he was a two-time All-American and won the Jim Thorpe Award as the nation's best defensive back in 1988. In baseball, he was a two-time All-ACC selection and was drafted by the Atlanta Braves in the second round of the 1988 MLB draft.

Sanders turned professional in 1989, signing with the Braves. He played for the Braves for three seasons, winning a World Series championship in 1992. In 1992, he also made his NFL debut with the Atlanta Falcons. He played for the Falcons for two seasons, before being traded to the San Francisco 49ers in 1994. With the 49ers, he won another Super Bowl championship in 1995.

Sanders continued to play both football and baseball for the next several seasons. He played for the Dallas Cowboys, Baltimore Ravens, and Washington Redskins in the NFL, and for the New York Yankees and Cincinnati Reds in MLB. He retired from baseball in 2001 and from football in 2004.

In addition to his on-field accomplishments, Sanders was also known for his flamboyant personality and his outspokenness. He was nicknamed "Prime Time" for his ability to make big plays in big games. He was also known for his unique fashion sense, which often included fur coats and flashy jewelry.

Sanders has been married twice. His first marriage, to Carolyn Chambers, lasted from 1989 to 1998. They had two children together,

Deion Jr. and Deiondra. His second marriage, to Pilar Biggers-Sanders, lasted from 1999 to 2013. They had three children together, Shilo, Shedeur, and Shelomi.

Sanders has been involved in several business ventures since retiring from sports. He has his own clothing line, a record label, and a restaurant. He is also a successful motivational speaker.

In 2020, Sanders was named the head football coach at Jackson State University. He led the team to two consecutive Celebration Bowl appearances and the first undefeated regular season in school history. In 2022, he was named the head football coach at the University of Colorado Boulder.

Sanders is a controversial figure, but there is no doubt that he is one of the most talented and accomplished athletes of all time. He is a true icon of sports and pop culture.

Here are some additional details about Deion Sanders' personal life:

* He is a devout Christian and has spoken openly about his faith.
* He is a philanthropist and has donated money to several charities.

* He is a mentor to young athletes and has spoken at several schools and youth organizations.

* He is a regular on the speaking circuit and has given motivational speeches to businesses and organizations around the world.

* He is a co-founder of the PrimeTime Foundation, which provides scholarships and mentoring to underprivileged youth.

Deion Sanders is a complex and fascinating figure. He is a talented athlete, a successful businessman, and a devoted family man. He is also a controversial figure, but there is no doubt that he is one of the most recognizable and influential people in the world.

CHAPTER SEVEN: Controversies

Deion Sanders is a Hall of Fame NFL player and coach who has never shied away from controversy. Here are some of the most notable controversies that have surrounded him:

His divorce from Pilar Sanders:

In 2011, Deion Sanders and his wife of 12 years, Pilar, divorced after a highly publicized and messy split. The couple had two sons together, and the divorce was reportedly acrimonious, with allegations of infidelity and domestic violence on both sides.

His relationship with Aleea Lee:

In the same year as his divorce, Deion Sanders was linked to a 19-year-old model named Aleea Lee. The photos of the two together were published in the media, and Sanders denied any wrongdoing, saying that he was simply helping Lee with her career.

His use of Twitter:

Deion Sanders is known for his outspokenness on Twitter, and he has often gotten himself into trouble with his tweets. In 2013, he was suspended from Twitter for a week after he made a series of offensive tweets about gay people.

His coaching style at Jackson State:

Deion Sanders was hired as the head coach of Jackson State University in 2020. He quickly became a polarizing figure, with some praising his innovative coaching methods and others criticizing his lack of experience. In 2023, he left Jackson State to take the head coaching job at the University of Colorado.

His use of religious imagery:

Deion Sanders is a devout Christian, and he has often used religious imagery in his coaching and public appearances. This has led to some controversy, with some people accusing him of trying to force his beliefs on others.

Despite the controversies, Deion Sanders remains a popular figure in the sports world. He is a charismatic and outspoken individual who is not afraid to speak his mind. His impact on the game of football is undeniable, and he will continue to be a source of discussion and debate for many years to come.

In addition to the controversies mentioned above, Deion Sanders has also been criticized for his lavish lifestyle and his tendency to make outlandish statements. However, he remains a popular figure among many fans, who admire his talent, his charisma, and his willingness to be himself.

Only time will tell what the future holds for Deion Sanders. However, one thing is for sure: he is a complex and controversial figure who is sure to continue to make headlines for years to come.

CONCLUSION

Deion Luwynn Sanders (born August 9, 1967), nicknamed "Prime Time" and "Neon Deion", is an American former professional football and baseball player who is the only person to have played in both a Super Bowl and a World Series. He played in the National Football League (NFL) for 14 seasons with the Atlanta Falcons, San Francisco 49ers, Dallas Cowboys, Washington Redskins, and Baltimore Ravens. Sanders was also a baseball outfielder for nine seasons in Major League Baseball (MLB) with the New York Yankees, Atlanta Braves, Cincinnati Reds, and San Francisco Giants.

Sanders was born in Fort Myers, Florida, and attended North Fort Myers High School, where he lettered in baseball, football, and track. He was a two-sport star in college, playing football and baseball at Florida State University. In football, he was a two-time All-American and won the Jim Thorpe Award as the nation's best defensive back in 1988. In baseball, he was a two-time All-ACC selection.

Sanders was drafted by the Atlanta Falcons in the fifth round of the 1989 NFL Draft. He quickly became one of the best cornerbacks in the league, earning All-Pro honors eight times and being named to the Pro Bowl ten times. He also returned punts and kickoffs for the

Falcons, setting a franchise record with 19 career touchdowns.

In 1992, Sanders signed with the New York Yankees, becoming the first player to play in both the NFL and MLB in the same season. He played in 27 games for the Yankees, hitting .221 with two home runs and 10 RBIs.

Sanders returned to the NFL in 1993 and played for the San Francisco 49ers. He helped the 49ers win Super Bowl XXIX, intercepting a pass in the game.

In 1994, Sanders signed with the Dallas Cowboys. He played for the Cowboys for six seasons, helping them win Super Bowl XXX.

Sanders signed with the Washington Redskins in 2000 and played for them for two seasons. He then signed with the Baltimore Ravens in 2004 and retired from the NFL after the 2005 season.

Sanders was inducted into the Pro Football Hall of Fame in 2011. He is also a member of the College Football Hall of Fame and the Florida Sports Hall of Fame.

In addition to his playing career, Sanders has also been a successful businessman and television personality. He has his own clothing line, a record label, and a sports marketing agency. He has also been a commentator for NFL and MLB games.

Sanders is known for his flamboyant personality and his love of fashion. He has been nicknamed "Prime Time" for his ability to make big plays on the field. He is also known for his flashy style, which often includes brightly colored suits and jewelry.

Sanders is a controversial figure, but he is also one of the most respected athletes in American history. He is a pioneer in the world of sports, and his accomplishments on the field and off the field are unmatched.

Made in the USA
Las Vegas, NV
19 December 2023